TAXES: HOW MODERN AMERICA IS RUINING YOUR INCOME

Copyright © 2024 by Tony Mandujano

All rights reserved. No part of this book may be reproduced, stored in a retrieval system, or transmitted by any means, electronic, mechanical, photocopying, recording, or otherwise, without the prior written permission of the publisher, except in the case of brief quotations embodied in critical articles and reviews.

Legal Notice

The information provided in this book is for general informational purposes only. While the author has made every effort to ensure the accuracy and completeness of the information contained herein, the author and publisher assume no responsibility for errors, omissions, inaccuracies, or any consequences arising from the use of this information. The reader is advised to verify any information and consult with a professional before making decisions based on the content of this book.

Disclaimer Notice

This book is intended to provide guidance and practical advice on taxes, and the modern take on how taxes are absurd, this is not a replacement or financial advice and replacement to any other type of financial or tax professional service. The author and publisher disclaim any liability arising directly or indirectly from the use of this book.

The practices and recommendations outlined in this book are based on the author's experiences and research. However, individual results may vary, and different circumstances may require different approaches. The reader is encouraged to exercise their own judgment and seek professional advice when needed.

By reading this book, you acknowledge and agree that the author and publisher are not responsible for any adverse effects or consequences resulting from the use or misuse of the information provided. The reader assumes full responsibility for their own actions and decisions.

JOIN THE COMMUNITY

Our community is filled with dozens of investors and people who are extremely knowledgeable of money and financial insight and taxes. Most community members are making $1,000 to $500,000 per day with huge business' and seasoned with business tax. Our community is private and consists of some of, if not the best, business owners/investors in the world.

Take a screenshot of QR Code ---> go into your Photos and hold down QR Image with your finger to use link or use your camera app over the QR Code to follow link

Praise for Economists

Milton Friedman:

- "Inflation is the one form of taxation that can be imposed without legislation."

Thomas Sowell:

- "It is amazing that people who think we cannot afford to pay for doctors, hospitals, and medication somehow think that we can afford to pay for doctors, hospitals, medication, and a government bureaucracy to administer it."

Will Rogers:

- "The income tax has made more liars out of the American people than golf has."

Arthur Laffer:

- "Higher taxes reduce the incentive to work and save, which is why in the 1970s, when taxes were so high, the economy grew slowly."

Robert Heinlein:

- "There is no worse tyranny than to force a man to pay for what he does not want merely because you think it would be good for him."

H.L. Mencken:

- "The government consists of a gang of men exactly like you and me. They have, taking one with another, no special talent for the business of government; they have only a talent for getting and holding office."

John Maynard Keynes:

- "The avoidance of taxes is the only intellectual pursuit that still carries any reward."

James Cook:

- "I am proud to be paying taxes in the United States. The only thing is – I could be just as proud for half the money."

Albert Einstein:

- "The hardest thing in the world to understand is the income tax."

Ronald Reagan:

- "The problem is not that people are taxed too little, the problem is that government spends too much."

Table of Contents

Part I: Introduction to the Taxation System

1. **Introduction: The Taxation Deception**
2. **The Birth of the Income Tax: A Historical Scam**
3. **Tax Code Complexity: Keeping You Confused on Purpose**

Part II: Direct Taxation and Its Impact

1. **Tax Brackets: Punishing Your Success**
2. **Withholding Woes: Your Paycheck Under Siege**

3. Payroll Taxes: Double Dipping into Your Earnings
4. Capital Gains Taxes: Penalizing Your Investments

Part III: Hidden and Indirect Taxes

1. Sales Tax: The Sneaky Wallet Drainer
2. Property Taxes: The Homeownership Trap
3. Estate Taxes: Death's Financial Sting
4. Gift Taxes: The Hidden Cost of Generosity
5. Hidden Taxes in Everyday Goods: The Invisible Hand in Your Pocket
6. Sin Taxes: Profiting from Your Vices
7. Tariffs and Trade Wars: The Secret Consumer Tax
8. Environmental Taxes: Greenwashing Your Wallet

Part IV: Corporate and Wealthy Tax Evasion

1. Loopholes for the Rich: The Legal Evaders
2. Corporate Tax Evasion: Multinational Manipulation
3. Subsidies for the Wealthy: Corporate Welfare Queens
4. The Offshore Tax Haven Scandal: Hiding Wealth Overseas

Part V: Specific Tax Challenges and Penalties

1. The AMT: The Alternative Minimum Trap
2. The Marriage Penalty: Taxing Your Union
3. Audit Anxiety: Living Under IRS Threat
4. Educational Impact: Student Loan Tax Deduction Deceptions
5. Healthcare Taxes: The Hidden Costs of Illness
6. The Cost of Tax Preparation: Paying to Pay Taxes

Part VI: Government and Legislative Influence

1. Government Waste: Funding Inefficiency with Your Money
2. Defense Spending: Tax Dollars into a Black Hole
3. Subsidies for the Wealthy: Corporate Welfare Queens
4. The Role of Lobbyists: Legislation for the Highest Bidder
5. Political Contributions and Tax Breaks: The Vicious Cycle
6. The Cost of Tax Enforcement: IRS Overreach

Part VII: Inequality and Social Impact

1. Fueling Income Inequality: The Unfair Tax Burden
2. Social Programs: Mismanagement of Your Contributions
3. Tax Reform Scams: Empty Promises and Real Costs
4. The Social Security Trust Fund Myth: Ponzi Scheme or Not?
5. The Flat Tax Fallacy: Simple Yet Deceptive
6. Whistleblowers' Plight: The Risk of Exposing Tax Fraud

Part VIII: Economic Sectors and Taxation

1. Small Business Taxation: Stifling Growth and Innovation
2. Freelancers and the Gig Economy: Navigating the Tax Minefield
3. Consumer Debt: Taxation's Role in the Vicious Cycle
4. The Underground Economy: Ignored and Untaxed Wealth

Part IX: Future and Emerging Tax Issues

1. Digital Economy Challenges: The Next Tax Frontier
2. Cryptocurrency Confusion: Taxing the Digital Revolution
3. Consumption Tax Proposals: Shifting the Burden
4. VAT vs. Sales Tax: Global Comparisons and Local Implications
5. Tax Evasion vs. Tax Avoidance: The Legal Grey Areas
6. Whistleblowers and the Fight Against Tax Fraud
7. Global Tax Coordination: Tackling International Tax Challenges
8. The Future of Work: Taxing Remote and Gig Workers
9. Environmental Taxes: Incentivizing Green Practices
10. The Aging Population: Tax Implications of Demographic Shifts

Part X: Why You Shouldn't Pay Taxes

1. The Moral Argument: Taxation as Theft
2. Historical Precedents for Tax Resistance
3. Inefficiency and Waste: Where Your Money Really Goes
4. Alternative Funding Models: Voluntary Contributions
5. The Right to Protest: Civil Disobedience and Taxes
6. The Case for Tax-Free Zones: Economic and Social Benefits
7. Tax Revolts: Historical and Modern Examples
8. The Psychological Impact: Stress and Financial Strain
9. The Hidden Costs: Compliance and Preparation
10. The Wealth Inequality Argument: Taxes Perpetuating Disparities
11. Sovereign Citizen Movement: A Radical Approach
12. The Path to Fair Taxation: Solutions and Reforms

Part XI: Conclusion and Solutions

1. Inflation and Taxes: Eroding Your Purchasing Power
2. Municipal Taxes: The Local Double Dip
3. State vs. Federal Taxes: Redundant and Burdensome
4. Tax Evasion vs. Tax Avoidance: The Legal Grey Areas
5. Conclusion: Finding a Path to Fair Taxation
6. Appendix: Resources and References

Part XII: Strategies for Minimizing Tax Burden

1. Business Ownership: Maximizing Deductions and Tax Benefits
2. Roth IRA: Tax-Free Growth and Withdrawals
3. Municipal Bonds: Tax-Free Interest Income
4. Capital Gains Taxes: Timing and Holding Periods

5. **Tax Loss Harvesting: Turning Losses into Gains**
6. **Buying a Home Using OPM (Other People's Money)**
7. **Home Sale Exemptions for Different Price Ranges**
8. **Depreciation: Cars, Homes, and Rental Property**
9. **Tax Returns with Children: Credits and Deductions**
10. **Best States for Taxes: Maximizing State Tax Benefits**
11. **State Tax Benefits: Taking Advantage of Each State**

Part I: Introduction to the Taxation System

Chapter 1: The Taxation Deception

Ladies and gentlemen, welcome to the show! Tonight, we're diving into the murky waters of what I like to call "The Taxation Deception." This isn't your average bedtime story – this is the tale of how the greatest illusionists of our time aren't magicians, but tax officials.

Let's take a trip back to the early 20th century. America is booming, the industrial revolution is in full swing, and suddenly, Uncle Sam decides he needs a piece of that prosperity pie. Enter the income tax. It was sold to the American people like a used car with a fresh coat of paint. "Don't worry," they said, "It's just a little tax. It'll only affect the super-rich." Fast forward a few years, and that "little tax" is knocking on everyone's door like an uninvited in-law.

The income tax was introduced with the 16th Amendment in 1913, promising to be a fair and simple way to fund the government. But here's the twist – what started as a manageable pamphlet has now ballooned into a monstrous beast. The tax code today is more complex than a Rubik's cube, and about as much fun to deal with. The complexity? It's no accident. If you can't convince them, confuse them. And confused we are! The tax code is so convoluted that even seasoned accountants need a map, a compass, and perhaps a prayer to navigate it.

Where does all this money go? The government portrays taxes as a necessary evil, the price we pay for a civilized society. Roads, schools, hospitals – all funded by our taxes. But, like any good thriller, there's a subplot. A chunk of that money vanishes into a black hole of inefficiency, waste, and some rather questionable expenses. Remember that time the Pentagon couldn't account for $21 trillion? That's right, trillion with a "T." It's like losing your car keys, if your car keys could buy you a small country.

So why do we keep playing along? Every year, we gather our receipts, W-2s, and 1099s, and dive into this madness. It's like a nationwide scavenger hunt, except instead of a prize, you get a bill. Awareness is the first step towards change. By understanding the depth of the deception, we can start to demand better – simpler, fairer taxes that don't feel like a rigged game.

Chapter 2: The Birth of the Income Tax: A Historical Scam

Ladies and gentlemen, let's travel back in time to the early 20th century, when the U.S. government pulled off one of the biggest scams in history: the introduction of the income tax. It's 1913, and the government decides it's time to tap into the burgeoning wealth of industrial America. But how do you sell a new tax to the American public? Easy, you promise them it'll only affect the super-rich. Sounds fair, right?

So, the 16th Amendment is passed, and the income tax is born. Initially, it was a modest tax, affecting only the top 1% of earners. But like any good horror story, the monster grew. The threshold for who had to pay dropped, and rates increased. What started as a tax on the wealthiest soon became a burden on the middle class and even the poor. The income tax was sold as a necessity for funding the government, but in reality, it was a Trojan horse. Once inside, it opened the gates for more taxes, more regulations, and more complexity.

Today, the tax code is a behemoth, a testament to over a century of bureaucratic expansion. The birth of the income tax was a historical scam, a bait-and-switch that hooked the American people and reeled us into a century-long trap. And like any good scam, it relied on our trust, our complacency, and our belief that it was for the greater good.

Chapter 3: Tax Code Complexity: Keeping You Confused on Purpose

Folks, let's talk about the tax code. If you've ever tried to read it, you know it's like diving into a novel written by Kafka after a bad day. The complexity isn't a bug – it's a feature. The more complicated it is, the harder it is for us to understand, let alone challenge.

Think about it: if the tax code were simple, we'd all know exactly what we owe and why. But instead, we have deductions, credits, exemptions, loopholes, and a million other little provisions that turn tax season into a nightmare. This complexity serves a purpose: it keeps us in the dark. The more confused we are, the less likely we are to notice when things don't add up.

Ever wonder why every year around tax time, software companies and tax preparers rake in billions? It's because the system is designed to be too complicated for the average person to handle alone. We're forced to rely on experts, who in turn have their own vested interests in keeping things just as they are.

So, while we're busy trying to figure out what form to fill out next, the government and the wealthy are playing a different game, one where they know all the rules and how to bend them. It's a system built on confusion, and as long as we stay baffled, they stay in control.

Chapter 4: Tax Brackets: Punishing Your Success

Now, let's dive into tax brackets. Sounds harmless enough, right? But here's the kicker: tax brackets are designed to punish success. As you climb the income ladder, you don't just pay more in taxes; you pay a higher percentage of your income in taxes. It's like a game where the better you play, the more the rules work against you.

Imagine running a marathon, and every time you pass a mile marker, someone hands you a heavier backpack. That's the tax bracket system. The more you earn, the higher percentage of your income gets siphoned off. It's progressive, they say, but in reality, it feels regressive to those who are just trying to get ahead.

The argument is that those who earn more should contribute more. Fair enough. But the way it's structured, it often feels like a penalty for doing well. Instead of encouraging success, it can discourage ambition. After all, why work harder if the government is just going to take a bigger slice of your pie?

And let's not forget about the so-called "marriage penalty." In some cases, two people earning separately might end up paying more taxes after they get married than they did individually. Love and taxes – both can be a bit of a gamble, it seems.

Chapter 5: Withholding Woes: Your Paycheck Under Siege

Ladies and gentlemen, let's talk about withholding taxes. Ah, yes, that little line on your paycheck that makes you wonder why you even bother getting out of bed in the morning. Withholding taxes are like a magician's trick – they make your money disappear before you even see it.

The idea behind withholding is simple: take the tax out of your paycheck before you have a chance to spend it. It's the government's way of ensuring they get their cut off the top. But here's the rub – by the time you see your paycheck, it's already been raided. And if you're not careful, you might end up owing even more come tax time.

Withholding is designed to be painless, to make tax payments seem like less of a burden. But in reality, it's a way to keep us from realizing just how much we're actually paying. If we had to write a check to the government every month, you can bet there'd be a lot more outrage. But by taking it out of our paychecks automatically, they keep us complacent.

And let's not forget the complexity of adjusting your withholding. Get it wrong, and you could either end up with a hefty tax bill or giving the government an interest-free loan. It's a system designed to keep us guessing, and all too often, we end up on the losing side of the equation.

Chapter 6: Payroll Taxes: Double Dipping into Your Earnings

Let's move on to payroll taxes. Now, payroll taxes are the silent killers of your paycheck. Social Security, Medicare – these are supposed to be safety nets for our future. But while we're paying into these programs, the government is double-dipping into our earnings.

Here's how it works: both you and your employer contribute to these taxes. Sounds fair, right? But in reality, it's all coming out of your potential earnings. If your employer didn't have to pay their share, that money could go into your paycheck. So, essentially, you're paying twice.

And let's talk about Social Security. We're told it's a trust fund, that our money is being saved for our retirement. But in reality, the funds we're paying now are being used to pay current retirees. It's a pay-as-you-go system, and as the population ages, the strain on this system is becoming more and more apparent.

Payroll taxes are one of the biggest expenses for the average worker, yet they're often overlooked because they're automatically deducted. It's another way the system keeps us in the dark, making sure we don't see the full picture of where our money is going.

Chapter 7: Capital Gains Taxes: Penalizing Your Investments

Finally, let's talk about capital gains taxes. Now, you might think investing your money is a smart move – and you'd be right. But the tax system has a way of turning your smart moves into a bit of a headache.

Capital gains taxes are the taxes you pay on the profit you make from selling an asset – stocks, real estate, what have you. The idea is that if you make money from an investment, you should pay a share of that profit to the government. Sounds reasonable, until you realize it's just another way the system penalizes you for being financially savvy.

Investing is supposed to be a way to grow your wealth, to plan for your future. But with capital gains taxes, a chunk of your hard-earned profits is taken away. It's like winning a game, only to have the referee take a portion of your prize.

And let's not forget the different rates for short-term and long-term gains. Hold an asset for less than a year, and you're hit with higher taxes. Hold it for longer, and you get a break. It's a system that rewards patience, sure, but also one that can be confusing and counterproductive for those trying to navigate the investment landscape.

In conclusion, folks, the tax system is a complex, often baffling maze designed to keep us in line and in the dark. But by shedding light on these deceptions, we can start to demand a fairer, more transparent system. So here's to understanding the game – may we one day see the rules change in our favor.

Part II: Direct Taxation and Its Impact

Chapter 4: Tax Brackets: Punishing Your Success

Ladies and gentlemen, let's dive into the deep end of the tax pool – tax brackets. Now, on the surface, tax brackets seem pretty straightforward. The more you make, the more you pay. But here's the kicker: tax brackets are designed to punish your success. As you climb the income ladder, you don't just pay more in taxes; you pay a higher percentage of your income in taxes. It's like running a marathon and being handed heavier and heavier backpacks at each mile marker.

Imagine you've just received a promotion and a nice pay raise. You're feeling on top of the world. But wait! Here comes the taxman, ready to take a bigger slice of your pie. Instead of celebrating your hard work and achievement, you're hit with a higher tax rate. It's progressive, they say, but in reality, it can feel regressive to those who are just trying to get ahead.

And let's talk about the so-called "marriage penalty." In some cases, two people earning separately might end up paying more taxes after they get married than they did individually. It's like the tax system is saying, "Congratulations on your wedding, now here's your bill." Love and taxes – both can be a bit of a gamble, it seems.

Chapter 5: Withholding Woes: Your Paycheck Under Siege

Folks, let's talk about withholding taxes. Ah, yes, that little line on your paycheck that makes you wonder why you even bother getting out of bed in the morning. Withholding taxes are like a magician's trick – they make your money disappear before you even see it.

The idea behind withholding is simple: take the tax out of your paycheck before you have a chance to spend it. It's the government's way of ensuring they get their cut off the top. But here's the rub – by the time you see your paycheck, it's already been raided. And if you're not careful, you might end up owing even more come tax time.

Withholding is designed to be painless, to make tax payments seem like less of a burden. But in reality, it's a way to keep us from realizing just how much we're actually paying. If we had to write a check to the government every month, you can bet there'd be a lot more outrage. But by taking it out of our paychecks automatically, they keep us complacent.

And let's not forget the complexity of adjusting your withholding. Get it wrong, and you could either end up with a hefty tax bill or giving the government an interest-free loan. It's a system designed to keep us guessing, and all too often, we end up on the losing side of the equation.

Chapter 6: Payroll Taxes: Double Dipping into Your Earnings

Let's move on to payroll taxes. Now, payroll taxes are the silent killers of your paycheck. Social Security, Medicare – these are supposed to be safety nets for our future. But while we're paying into these programs, the government is double-dipping into our earnings.

Here's how it works: both you and your employer contribute to these taxes. Sounds fair, right? But in reality, it's all coming out of your potential earnings. If your employer didn't have to pay their share, that money could go into your paycheck. So, essentially, you're paying twice.

And let's talk about Social Security. We're told it's a trust fund, that our money is being saved for our retirement. But in reality, the funds we're paying now are being used to pay current retirees. It's a pay-as-you-go system, and as the population ages, the strain on this system is becoming more and more apparent.

Payroll taxes are one of the biggest expenses for the average worker, yet they're often overlooked because they're automatically deducted. It's another way the system keeps us in the dark, making sure we don't see the full picture of where our money is going.

Chapter 7: Capital Gains Taxes: Penalizing Your Investments

Finally, let's talk about capital gains taxes. Now, you might think investing your money is a smart move – and you'd be right. But the tax system has a way of turning your smart moves into a bit of a headache.

Capital gains taxes are the taxes you pay on the profit you make from selling an asset – stocks, real estate, what have you. The idea is that if you make money from an investment, you should pay a share of that profit to the government. Sounds reasonable, until you realize it's just another way the system penalizes you for being financially savvy.

Investing is supposed to be a way to grow your wealth, to plan for your future. But with capital gains taxes, a chunk of your hard-earned profits is taken away. It's like winning a game, only to have the referee take a portion of your prize.

And let's not forget the different rates for short-term and long-term gains. Hold an asset for less than a year, and you're hit with higher taxes. Hold it for longer, and you get a break. It's a system that rewards patience, sure, but also one that can be confusing and counterproductive for those trying to navigate the investment landscape.

Chapter 8: Sales Tax: The Sneaky Wallet Drainer

Ladies and gentlemen, let's talk about sales tax – the sneaky wallet drainer. Sales tax is like a stealth bomber, swooping in and taking a bite out of your wallet every time you make a purchase. You go to buy a cup of coffee, a new pair of shoes, or even a car, and bam! There's that extra charge.

Sales tax is insidious because it's a tax on consumption. The more you buy, the more you pay. It hits everyone, but it's especially hard on those with lower incomes who spend a larger portion of their earnings on essentials. It's a regressive tax in disguise, taking a bigger chunk out of the wallets of those who can least afford it.

And here's the kicker – sales tax rates vary by state, and even by city. So, you could be paying more or less depending on where you live. It's like a lottery, but instead of winning money, you're losing it. It's another way the tax system keeps us on our toes, constantly reaching into our pockets.

Chapter 9: Property Taxes: The Homeownership Trap

Now, let's discuss property taxes – the homeownership trap. You've worked hard, saved up, and bought your dream home. But the taxman isn't far behind. Property taxes are like an annual subscription fee for owning a piece of the American dream.

Property taxes are based on the value of your home, but here's the catch – property values can fluctuate wildly. One year your home's worth a fortune, the next it's plummeted, but your taxes don't always reflect that. It's like playing the stock market, but with your most valuable asset.

And let's not forget how property taxes can drive people out of their homes. As neighborhoods gentrify and property values rise, long-time residents can find themselves priced out by skyrocketing taxes. It's a cruel twist, where improving your community can mean losing your home.

Chapter 10: Estate Taxes: Death's Financial Sting

Ladies and gentlemen, let's talk about estate taxes – death's financial sting. You've worked hard all your life, built up a nest egg, and planned to leave something for your loved ones. But when you pass away, the taxman comes knocking.

Estate taxes are like a final insult. After a lifetime of paying taxes, the government takes another bite out of your estate when you die. It's like they're saying, "You can't take it with you, but we'll make sure you don't leave much behind either."

And here's the kicker – estate taxes don't just affect the ultra-wealthy. As property values and the cost of living rise, more and more middle-class families find themselves subject to these taxes. It's another way the tax system reaches into our pockets, even after we're gone.

Chapter 11: Gift Taxes: The Hidden Cost of Generosity

Now, let's discuss gift taxes – the hidden cost of generosity. You'd think giving a gift would be a simple act of kindness, but the taxman has other ideas. Gift taxes are designed to prevent people from avoiding estate taxes by giving away their assets before they die.

But here's the rub – the rules are complicated, and the limits change every year. It's like trying to play a game where the rules are constantly shifting. If you give too much, you could end up owing taxes on your generosity. It's another way the system makes sure it gets its cut, no matter how you try to distribute your wealth.

Chapter 12: Hidden Taxes in Everyday Goods: The Invisible Hand in Your Pocket

Ladies and gentlemen, let's talk about hidden taxes in everyday goods – the invisible hand in your pocket. You might not see them, but they're there, lurking in the price of almost everything you buy. From gas to groceries, hidden taxes are everywhere.

These taxes are built into the price of goods and services, so you're paying them without even realizing it. It's a stealthy way for the government to collect revenue without raising obvious alarms. And because these taxes are hidden, we often don't realize just how much we're paying.

Take gasoline, for example. A significant portion of the price at the pump is made up of taxes. Every time you fill up, you're contributing to government coffers. The same goes for utilities, alcohol, and tobacco. It's like being nickeled and dimed to death.

Chapter 13: Sin Taxes: Profiting from Your Vices

Now, let's discuss sin taxes – profiting from your vices. Sin taxes are levied on goods deemed harmful, like alcohol, tobacco, and sugary drinks. The idea is to discourage unhealthy behavior while generating revenue. But here's the kicker – these taxes are often more about money than morality.

Sin taxes disproportionately affect lower-income individuals, who are more likely to consume these products. It's a regressive tax, hitting hardest those who can least afford it. And while the stated goal is to improve public health, the revenue generated is often used to plug budget holes rather than fund health initiatives.

Chapter 14: Tariffs and Trade Wars: The Secret Consumer Tax

Ladies and gentlemen, let's talk about tariffs and trade wars – the secret consumer tax. Tariffs are taxes on imported goods, meant to protect domestic industries. But here's the twist – while they're paid by importers, the cost is often passed on to consumers.

When tariffs are imposed, the price of imported goods rises. And because many products are made with imported components, the cost of domestic goods can increase as well. It's a hidden tax that hits your wallet every time you shop.

Trade wars, where countries retaliate with tariffs of their own, can escalate this hidden tax. Prices rise, and the economy suffers. It's a game of geopolitical chicken, and we're the ones paying the price.

Chapter 15: Environmental Taxes: Greenwashing Your Wallet

Finally, let's discuss environmental taxes – greenwashing your wallet. Environmental taxes are designed to reduce pollution and promote sustainability. They sound great in theory, but in practice, they often end up as another way to siphon money from our pockets.

Take carbon taxes, for example. The idea is to reduce greenhouse gas emissions by making it more expensive to pollute. But the cost is often passed on to consumers in the form of higher prices for goods and services. It's another hidden tax that hits us where it hurts.

And let's not forget the complexity of these taxes. Rebates, credits, and exemptions make it hard to know what you're actually paying. It's a system designed to look green on the surface, but underneath, it's just another way to generate revenue.

In conclusion, folks, direct taxation and its many forms are designed to keep us paying, often without us even realizing how much. By understanding these hidden costs, we can start to demand a fairer, more transparent system. So here's to uncovering the truth – may we one day see a tax system that works for everyone.

Part III: Hidden and Indirect Taxes

Chapter 16: Loopholes for the Rich: The Legal Evaders

Ladies and gentlemen, let's kick off with a topic that's sure to get you riled up – loopholes for the rich. Ah yes, the legal way to dodge taxes. It's like a VIP pass that says, "Rules don't apply to me."

You see, while the average Joe is busy slogging through tax forms, the wealthy have an army of accountants and lawyers finding ways to minimize their tax bill. These loopholes are written into the tax code, often by lawmakers who benefit from them, or their wealthy benefactors. It's like they're playing chess while the rest of us are stuck on checkers.

One of the most notorious is the carried interest loophole. This allows hedge fund managers to pay taxes on their income at a lower capital gains rate rather than as ordinary income. It's as if they've found a secret door that leads straight to tax savings. And let's not forget offshore tax havens. Wealthy individuals and corporations stash their money in places like the Cayman Islands, avoiding US taxes. It's like they've found a hidden island where taxes don't exist. Meanwhile, we're left to pick up the tab.

Chapter 17: Corporate Tax Evasion: Multinational Manipulation

Now, let's talk about corporate tax evasion – the art of multinational manipulation. Corporations are supposed to pay taxes just like the rest of us, right? But many of them have turned tax evasion into an art form.

Through clever accounting tricks and exploiting loopholes, multinational corporations shift their profits to low-tax or no-tax jurisdictions. It's called profit shifting, and it's a way to make their money disappear from the eyes of the IRS. For example, a company might set up a subsidiary in a tax haven and then shift its profits there through complex transactions and transfer pricing. It's all legal, but it's also a way to dodge paying their fair share.

And while these corporations are enjoying their tax holidays, the rest of us are left to make up the difference. It's like going out to dinner with a friend who always conveniently forgets their wallet.

Chapter 18: Subsidies for the Wealthy: Corporate Welfare Queens

Ladies and gentlemen, let's dive into the murky world of subsidies for the wealthy – the corporate welfare queens. Now, subsidies are supposed to help struggling industries and promote economic growth. But in reality, they often end up lining the pockets of the rich.

Take the fossil fuel industry, for example. Despite being one of the most profitable sectors in the world, it receives billions in government subsidies. It's like giving a billionaire a discount on their yacht. These subsidies are supposed to promote energy independence and job creation, but they often end up as corporate welfare.

And let's not forget about the tech giants. Companies like Amazon and Google receive massive tax breaks and subsidies to build new facilities. It's as if they need more help to make money. Meanwhile, small businesses and regular folks are left to fend for themselves.

Chapter 19: The Offshore Tax Haven Scandal: Hiding Wealth Overseas

Now, let's discuss the offshore tax haven scandal – hiding wealth overseas. Offshore tax havens are like the secret hideouts of the rich and powerful, where their money can relax, sip a cocktail, and avoid the taxman.

These havens offer low or no taxes, banking secrecy, and minimal regulations. It's like a financial paradise for those who can afford to get there. Wealthy individuals and corporations move their money to these havens to avoid paying taxes in their home countries. It's perfectly legal, but it's also perfectly unfair.

The money hidden in offshore tax havens is staggering – trillions of dollars that could be used to fund schools, hospitals, and infrastructure. Instead, it's sitting in secret bank accounts, out of reach of the tax authorities. It's like a giant game of hide and seek, and we're all losing.

Chapter 20: The AMT: The Alternative Minimum Trap

Ladies and gentlemen, let's talk about the Alternative Minimum Tax, or AMT – the trap for those who thought they could escape. The AMT was designed to ensure that wealthy individuals and corporations paid at least a minimum amount of tax, regardless of how many deductions or credits they claimed.

But here's the kicker – over time, the AMT started to affect middle-class taxpayers as well. It's like setting a trap for a lion and catching a house cat instead. The AMT requires taxpayers to calculate their taxes twice – once under the regular tax system and once under the AMT. Then they pay the higher amount. It's a complicated and time-consuming process that adds stress and confusion to tax season.

And while the AMT was intended to close loopholes, it often ends up creating new headaches for taxpayers who are just trying to play by the rules. It's like a maze with no exit, designed to keep us running in circles.

Chapter 21: The Marriage Penalty: Taxing Your Union

Now, let's discuss the marriage penalty – taxing your union. You'd think that getting married would come with financial benefits, but in the world of taxes, it's often the opposite. The marriage penalty occurs when a married couple ends up paying more in taxes than they would as two single individuals. It's like the tax system's way of saying, "Congratulations on your wedding, now here's your bill."

This happens because the tax brackets for married couples aren't always double those for single filers. So, if both spouses earn a significant income, they can end up in a higher tax bracket. It's a quirk of the tax code that can turn wedded bliss into financial stress.

And it's not just the federal tax code – state and local taxes can also contribute to the marriage penalty. It's like the system is punishing you for finding love and stability.

Chapter 22: Audit Anxiety: Living Under IRS Threat

Ladies and gentlemen, let's talk about audit anxiety – living under the constant threat of the IRS. The thought of an IRS audit is enough to keep anyone up at night. It's like the taxman's version of a horror movie, where the monster is a pile of paperwork and the suspense never ends.

An audit can be triggered for a variety of reasons – high deductions, complex financial transactions, or even just random selection. Once you're in the IRS's sights, it's a deep dive into your financial life. It's like having a magnifying glass put to every receipt and bank statement.

The process is stressful, time-consuming, and can be costly if you need to hire a professional to help you navigate it. And even if you've done everything by the book, the fear of making a mistake can be overwhelming. It's a system designed to keep us in line, and the threat of an audit is its biggest stick.

Chapter 23: Educational Impact: Student Loan Tax Deduction Deceptions

Now, let's discuss the educational impact – student loan tax deduction deceptions. Student loans are supposed to be an investment in your future, but the tax code has a way of making you pay twice. While there are deductions for student loan interest, they come with limitations and restrictions.

The student loan interest deduction allows you to deduct up to $2,500 of interest paid on student loans. But here's the catch – the deduction phases out as your income increases. So, if you're making a decent salary, you might not qualify. It's like rewarding you for getting an education and then penalizing you for putting it to good use.

And let's not forget the complexity of claiming this deduction. The rules can be confusing, and if you make a mistake, it can cost you. It's another way the tax system adds stress to an already difficult financial situation.

Chapter 24: Healthcare Taxes: The Hidden Costs of Illness

Ladies and gentlemen, let's talk about healthcare taxes – the hidden costs of illness. Healthcare in America is expensive enough without the added burden of taxes. But the tax system has a way of making sure you pay, even when you're sick.

There are taxes on everything from medical devices to insurance premiums. And while there are deductions for medical expenses, they come with high thresholds and complex rules. You can only deduct medical expenses that exceed 7.5% of your adjusted gross income. It's like a tax system designed to kick you when you're down.

And let's not forget the penalty for not having health insurance, known as the individual mandate. While the penalty was reduced to zero in 2019, it was a tax on those who could least afford health insurance. It's like the tax system's way of saying, "Can't afford to be healthy? Here's a fine."

Chapter 25: The Cost of Tax Preparation: Paying to Pay Taxes

Finally, let's discuss the cost of tax preparation – paying to pay taxes. The tax code is so complex that most of us need help to navigate it. Enter the tax preparation industry, ready to help you file your taxes – for a fee, of course.

Americans spend billions of dollars each year on tax preparation services and software. It's a hidden cost of our complicated tax system. We're paying to pay our taxes. It's like hiring a guide to help you through a maze, a maze that didn't need to be so complicated in the first place.

And let's not forget about the time we spend. The IRS estimates that the average taxpayer spends 13 hours preparing their taxes. That's time we could be spending with our families, working, or doing just about anything else. It's a system designed to take not just our money, but our time and peace of mind as well.

In conclusion, folks, hidden and indirect taxes are designed to keep us paying, often without us even realizing how much. By understanding these hidden costs, we can start to demand a fairer, more transparent system. So here's to uncovering the truth – may we one day see a tax system that works for everyone.

Part IV: Corporate and Wealthy Tax Evasion

Chapter 26: Loopholes for the Rich: The Legal Evaders

Ladies and gentlemen, let's start with a hot topic – loopholes for the rich. Yes, the legal evaders who have turned tax avoidance into an art form. Imagine playing Monopoly where some players can skip past "Go" without paying a cent, while the rest of us are stuck mortgaging Baltic Avenue.

The wealthy have access to a toolbox full of tax tricks that most of us can only dream of. Fancy a yacht? Just call it a business expense. Own a jet? Write it off as a necessity for your multinational empire. It's like having a cheat code for life. The carried interest loophole, for example, allows hedge fund managers to pay lower taxes on their earnings by treating them as long-term capital gains instead of regular income. This loophole alone saves them billions of dollars, while you and I are left wondering if we can deduct our Netflix subscription because, technically, we need to relax to work better, right?

And let's not forget the magic of tax credits for things like historical building renovations. Sure, it's nice to preserve history, but when billionaires get huge tax breaks for restoring their own properties, it starts to feel less like philanthropy and more like self-serving preservation of their wealth.

Chapter 27: Corporate Tax Evasion: Multinational Manipulation

Now, let's talk about corporate tax evasion – the craft of multinational manipulation. Corporations are supposed to pay their share of taxes just like the rest of us, but many have turned tax evasion into a strategic business operation.

Through a web of subsidiaries, complex financial transactions, and accounting gymnastics, multinational corporations shift their profits to low-tax or no-tax jurisdictions. It's called profit shifting, and it's like sending your money on a luxury vacation where taxes don't exist. For example, a tech giant might set up a subsidiary in Ireland, known for its favorable tax rates, and funnel its profits through there to avoid the higher taxes at home.

The most infuriating part? These corporations often benefit from the infrastructure and services funded by the very taxes they avoid. It's like throwing a party in someone else's house and then sneaking out without paying for the cleanup. And while these corporations are enjoying their tax-free holidays, the rest of us are left to cover the costs, wondering why our roads are full of potholes and our public schools are underfunded.

Chapter 28: Subsidies for the Wealthy: Corporate Welfare Queens

Ladies and gentlemen, let's dive into the murky waters of subsidies for the wealthy – the corporate welfare queens. Subsidies are supposed to help struggling industries and promote economic growth, but all too often, they end up padding the pockets of the rich.

Take the fossil fuel industry, for example. Despite being one of the most profitable sectors in the world, it receives billions in government subsidies. It's like giving a multimillionaire a discount on their yacht fuel. These subsidies are justified in the name of energy independence and job creation, but they often end up as corporate welfare, distorting markets and propping up industries that don't need the help.

And let's not forget the tech giants. Companies like Amazon and Google receive massive tax breaks and subsidies to build new facilities. It's as if they need more help to make money. These corporations are already immensely profitable, yet they benefit from taxpayer-funded incentives while small businesses struggle to keep their doors open. It's like watching Goliath get a new slingshot while David is left to fend for himself with a rock.

Chapter 29: The Offshore Tax Haven Scandal: Hiding Wealth Overseas

Now, let's discuss the offshore tax haven scandal – hiding wealth overseas. Offshore tax havens are like the secret hideouts of the rich and powerful, where their money can relax, sip a cocktail, and avoid the taxman.

These havens offer low or no taxes, banking secrecy, and minimal regulations. It's like a financial paradise for those who can afford to get there. Wealthy individuals and corporations move their money to these havens to avoid paying taxes in their home countries. It's perfectly legal, but it's also perfectly unfair.

The money hidden in offshore tax havens is staggering – trillions of dollars that could be used to fund schools, hospitals, and infrastructure. Instead, it's sitting in secret bank accounts, out of reach of the tax authorities. It's like a giant game of hide and seek, and we're all losing. These offshore maneuvers create a massive tax gap, where the wealthy escape their tax obligations, leaving the rest of us to pick up the slack.

Chapter 30: The AMT: The Alternative Minimum Trap

Ladies and gentlemen, let's talk about the Alternative Minimum Tax, or AMT – the trap for those who thought they could escape. The AMT was designed to ensure that wealthy individuals and corporations paid at least a minimum amount of tax, regardless of how many deductions or credits they claimed.

But here's the kicker – over time, the AMT started to affect middle-class taxpayers as well. It's like setting a trap for a lion and catching a house cat instead. The AMT requires taxpayers to calculate their taxes twice – once under the regular tax system and once under the AMT. Then they pay the higher amount. It's a complicated and time-consuming process that adds stress and confusion to tax season.

And while the AMT was intended to close loopholes and ensure fairness, it often ends up creating new headaches for taxpayers who are just trying to play by the rules. It's like a maze with no exit, designed to keep us running in circles.

Chapter 31: The Marriage Penalty: Taxing Your Union

Now, let's discuss the marriage penalty – taxing your union. You'd think that getting married would come with financial benefits, but in the world of taxes, it's often the opposite. The marriage penalty occurs when a married couple ends up paying more in taxes than they would as two single individuals. It's like the tax system's way of saying, "Congratulations on your wedding, now here's your bill."

This happens because the tax brackets for married couples aren't always double those for single filers. So, if both spouses earn a significant income, they can end up in a higher tax bracket. It's a quirk of the tax code that can turn wedded bliss into financial stress. It's particularly tough on dual-income couples where both partners are high earners. Instead of enjoying the financial benefits of a combined income, they find themselves facing a larger tax bill.

Chapter 32: Audit Anxiety: Living Under IRS Threat

Ladies and gentlemen, let's talk about audit anxiety – living under the constant threat of the IRS. The thought of an IRS audit is enough to keep anyone up at night. It's like the taxman's version of a horror movie, where the monster is a pile of paperwork and the suspense never ends.

An audit can be triggered for a variety of reasons – high deductions, complex financial transactions, or even just random selection. Once you're in the IRS's sights, it's a deep dive into your financial life. It's like having a magnifying glass put to every receipt and bank statement.

The process is stressful, time-consuming, and can be costly if you need to hire a professional to help you navigate it. And even if you've done everything by the book, the fear of making a mistake can be overwhelming. It's a system designed to keep us in line, and the threat of an audit is its biggest stick. The fear of an audit looms large, making us second-guess every deduction and expense. It's a climate of fear that ensures compliance, but at what cost to our peace of mind?

Chapter 33: Educational Impact: Student Loan Tax Deduction Deceptions

Now, let's discuss the educational impact – student loan tax deduction deceptions. Student loans are supposed to be an investment in your future, but the tax code has a way of making you pay twice. While there are deductions for student loan interest, they come with limitations and restrictions.

The student loan interest deduction allows you to deduct up to $2,500 of interest paid on student loans. But here's the catch – the deduction phases out as your income increases. So, if you're making a decent salary, you might not qualify. It's like rewarding you for getting an education and then penalizing you for putting it to good use.

And let's not forget the complexity of claiming this deduction. The rules can be confusing, and if you make a mistake, it can cost you. It's another way the tax system adds stress to an already difficult financial situation. The dream of a better future through education comes with a price tag that keeps growing, long after graduation.

Chapter 34: Healthcare Taxes: The Hidden Costs of Illness

Ladies and gentlemen, let's talk about healthcare taxes – the hidden costs of illness. Healthcare in America is expensive enough without the added burden of taxes. But the tax system has a way of making sure you pay, even when you're sick.

There are taxes on everything from medical devices to insurance premiums. And while there are deductions for medical expenses, they come with high thresholds and complex rules. You can only deduct medical expenses that exceed 7.5% of your adjusted gross income. It's like a tax system designed to kick you when you're down.

And let's not forget the penalty for not having health insurance, known as the individual mandate. While the penalty was reduced to zero in 2019, it was a tax on those who could least afford health insurance. It's like the tax system's way of saying, "Can't afford to be healthy? Here's a fine." The financial burden of illness is compounded by a tax system that seems to penalize those who are already struggling the most.

Chapter 35: The Cost of Tax Preparation: Paying to Pay Taxes

Finally, let's discuss the cost of tax preparation – paying to pay taxes. The tax code is so complex that most of us need help to navigate it. Enter the tax preparation industry, ready to help you file your taxes – for a fee, of course.

Americans spend billions of dollars each year on tax preparation services and software. It's a hidden cost of our complicated tax system. We're paying to pay our taxes. It's like hiring a guide to help you through a maze, a maze that didn't need to be so complicated in the first place.

And let's not forget about the time we spend. The IRS estimates that the average taxpayer spends 13 hours preparing their taxes. That's time we could be spending with our families, working, or doing just about anything else. It's a system designed to take not just our money, but our time and peace of mind as well. The frustration of tax season is amplified by the realization that the complexity of the system benefits an entire industry dedicated to helping us navigate it.

In conclusion, folks, corporate and wealthy tax evasion schemes are designed to keep the rich richer and the rest of us footing the bill. By understanding these tactics, we can start to demand a fairer, more transparent system. So here's to uncovering the truth – may we one day see a tax system that works for everyone.

Part V: Specific Tax Challenges and Penalties

Chapter 36: The AMT: The Alternative Minimum Trap

Ladies and gentlemen, let's dive into the world of the Alternative Minimum Tax, or AMT – a classic case of the government's "gotcha!" The AMT was introduced to ensure that high-income earners pay at least a minimum level of tax, no matter how many deductions they claim. Sounds fair, right? But here's the kicker – it's ended up trapping more than just the super-rich.

Imagine you're a middle-class worker who's scrimped and saved, taken all the right deductions, and suddenly, you're hit with the AMT. The rules require you to calculate your taxes twice: once under the regular tax system and once under the AMT, and then pay the higher amount. It's like going through an obstacle course twice and then being told you didn't quite make it.

The AMT doesn't adjust for inflation, so over the years, more and more middle-class families have been caught in its web. It's as if the lion trap was set, but it's the house cats that keep getting snagged. This tax trap adds stress and confusion to tax season, leaving many to wonder if they'll ever find a way out.

Chapter 37: The Marriage Penalty: Taxing Your Union

Now, let's talk about the marriage penalty – the tax system's way of punishing love. You'd think tying the knot would bring financial perks, but in many cases, getting married can actually increase your tax bill. It's as if the tax system is saying, "Congratulations on your wedding, now here's your bill."

The marriage penalty occurs when a married couple ends up paying more in taxes than they would as two single individuals. This happens because the tax brackets for married couples aren't always double those for single filers. So if both spouses earn a significant income, they can find themselves pushed into a higher tax bracket.

This quirk of the tax code can turn what should be a joyous occasion into a financial headache. Instead of enjoying the benefits of a combined income, couples are left juggling a larger tax bill. It's like getting a wedding present from the IRS – and it's always a bill.

Chapter 38: Audit Anxiety: Living Under IRS Threat

Ladies and gentlemen, let's address audit anxiety – that gnawing fear that the IRS might come knocking. An IRS audit is like a surprise pop quiz you're never prepared for, complete with a deep dive into your financial history.

Audits can be triggered for various reasons: high deductions, complex financial transactions, or even just random selection. Once you're in the IRS's crosshairs, it's a detailed examination of your financial life, every receipt, and every bank statement under the microscope.

The process is stressful, time-consuming, and can be expensive if you need to hire professional help. Even if you've done everything by the book, the fear of making a mistake can be overwhelming. It's a system designed to keep us in line, with the threat of an audit serving as the ultimate stick.

Chapter 39: Educational Impact: Student Loan Tax Deduction Deceptions

Let's discuss the educational impact – student loan tax deduction deceptions. Student loans are supposed to be an investment in your future, but the tax system has a way of making you pay twice. While there are deductions for student loan interest, they come with limitations and restrictions that can feel like a cruel joke.

The student loan interest deduction allows you to deduct up to $2,500 of interest paid on student loans. But here's the catch – the deduction phases out as your income increases. So, if you're making a decent salary, you might not qualify. It's like rewarding you for getting an education and then penalizing you for putting it to good use.

The rules for claiming this deduction can be confusing, and if you make a mistake, it can cost you. It's another way the tax system adds stress to an already difficult financial situation. The dream of a better future through education comes with a price tag that keeps growing long after graduation.

Chapter 40: Healthcare Taxes: The Hidden Costs of Illness

Ladies and gentlemen, let's delve into healthcare taxes – the hidden costs of illness. Healthcare in America is expensive enough without the added burden of taxes. But the tax system has a way of making sure you pay, even when you're sick.

There are taxes on everything from medical devices to insurance premiums. And while there are deductions for medical expenses, they come with high thresholds and complex rules. You can only deduct medical expenses that exceed 7.5% of your adjusted gross income. It's like a tax system designed to kick you when you're down.

And let's not forget the penalty for not having health insurance, known as the individual mandate. While the penalty was reduced to zero in 2019, it was a tax on those who could least afford health insurance. It's like the tax system's way of saying, "Can't afford to be healthy? Here's a fine." The financial burden of illness is compounded by a tax system that seems to penalize those who are already struggling the most.

Chapter 41: The Cost of Tax Preparation: Paying to Pay Taxes

Now, let's discuss the cost of tax preparation – paying to pay taxes. The tax code is so complex that most of us need help to navigate it. Enter the tax preparation industry, ready to help you file your taxes – for a fee, of course.

Americans spend billions of dollars each year on tax preparation services and software. It's a hidden cost of our complicated tax system. We're paying to pay our taxes. It's like hiring a guide to help you through a maze, a maze that didn't need to be so complicated in the first place.

And let's not forget about the time we spend. The IRS estimates that the average taxpayer spends 13 hours preparing their taxes. That's time we could be spending with our families, working, or doing just about anything else. It's a system designed to take not just our money, but our time and peace of mind as well. The frustration of tax season is amplified by the realization that the complexity of the system benefits an entire industry dedicated to helping us navigate it.

Chapter 42: The Social Security Trust Fund Myth: Ponzi Scheme or Not?

Ladies and gentlemen, let's talk about the Social Security Trust Fund – is it a safeguard for our future or a cleverly disguised Ponzi scheme? We're told that our Social Security contributions are being saved in a trust fund for our retirement. But the reality is much murkier.

The money we pay into Social Security is used to pay current retirees, with any surplus being borrowed by the federal government to cover other expenses. It's a pay-as-you-go system, and as the population ages, the strain on this system becomes more and more apparent.

There's a real fear that Social Security won't be able to meet its obligations in the future, leaving younger generations wondering if they'll ever see a return on their contributions. It's like putting your money into a retirement plan, only to find out it's being spent faster than it's being saved.

Chapter 43: Government Waste: Funding Inefficiency with Your Money

Now, let's discuss government waste – funding inefficiency with your money. Every year, billions of dollars in taxpayer money are wasted on inefficient programs, redundant projects, and outright fraud. It's like watching your hard-earned cash go down the drain.

From overpriced military contracts to unnecessary government buildings, the list of wasteful spending is endless. And while some waste is inevitable in any large organization, the scale of government waste is staggering. It's like handing your money to someone with a hole in their pocket and watching it trickle away.

Chapter 44: Defense Spending: Tax Dollars into a Black Hole

Ladies and gentlemen, let's talk about defense spending – a black hole for tax dollars. The United States spends more on its military than the next ten countries combined. While a strong defense is crucial, the sheer scale of spending raises questions about efficiency and necessity.

Overpriced contracts, failed weapons systems, and unaccounted-for funds are just a few examples of how defense spending can spiral out of control. It's like writing a blank check and hoping it's spent wisely, but often finding out it's been squandered.

Chapter 45: Subsidies for the Wealthy: Corporate Welfare Queens

Let's revisit subsidies for the wealthy – the corporate welfare queens. We've already touched on this in Part IV, but it's worth reiterating how these subsidies distort the market and benefit the rich at the expense of the average taxpayer.

While subsidies are supposed to promote economic growth, they often end up as handouts to already profitable corporations. It's like giving a billionaire a bonus check while the rest of us struggle to make ends meet.

Chapter 46: The Role of Lobbyists: Legislation for the Highest Bidder

Now, let's discuss the role of lobbyists – legislation for the highest bidder. Lobbyists are paid to influence lawmakers on behalf of special interest groups. And while lobbying is a legitimate part of the political process, it often skews legislation in favor of those with the deepest pockets.

From tax breaks for specific industries to loopholes for the wealthy, lobbyists ensure that the tax code is written with their clients in mind. It's like having a rulebook where the richest players get to make the rules. This creates a system where the needs of ordinary citizens are often overshadowed by the interests of the powerful.

Chapter 47: Political Contributions and Tax Breaks: The Vicious Cycle

Ladies and gentlemen, let's talk about political contributions and tax breaks – the vicious cycle. Political contributions buy influence, and that influence often results in tax breaks for the contributors. It's a pay-to-play system that undermines democracy and fairness.

Corporations and wealthy individuals donate large sums to political campaigns, and in return, they receive favorable tax treatment. It's like a revolving door where money and power circulate, leaving the rest of us outside looking in. This cycle perpetuates inequality and ensures that the tax code remains skewed in favor of the rich.

Chapter 48: The Cost of Tax Enforcement: IRS Overreach

Finally, let's discuss the cost of tax enforcement – IRS overreach. The IRS is tasked with collecting taxes and ensuring compliance, but their methods can sometimes feel heavy-handed and invasive.

From aggressive audits to harsh penalties, the IRS's tactics can leave taxpayers feeling like they're under siege. It's like having a watchdog that occasionally bites the hand that feeds it. While tax enforcement is necessary, there's a fine line between ensuring compliance and overstepping boundaries.

In conclusion, folks, the specific tax challenges and penalties we face are designed to keep us paying and in line. By understanding these issues, we can start to demand a fairer, more transparent system. So here's to uncovering the truth – may we one day see a tax system that works for everyone.

Part VI: Government and Legislative Influence

Chapter 49: Government Waste: Funding Inefficiency with Your Money

Ladies and gentlemen, let's dive into the murky waters of government waste – funding inefficiency with your money. Every year, billions of taxpayer dollars are wasted on inefficient programs, redundant projects, and outright fraud. It's like watching your hard-earned cash get thrown into a bonfire.

From overpriced military contracts to unnecessary government buildings, the list of wasteful spending is endless. It's like handing your money to someone with a hole in their pocket and watching it trickle away. And let's not forget the countless reports of lavish conferences, duplicate programs, and unaccounted-for expenses. The government is like a leaky ship, and we're the ones bailing out water with our wallets.

But what makes it even more infuriating is the lack of accountability. Projects go over budget, timelines get extended, and yet, no one seems to bear the consequences. It's like being stuck in a bad reality show where incompetence reigns supreme, and we're all paying the price.

Chapter 50: Defense Spending: Tax Dollars into a Black Hole

Now, let's talk about defense spending – a black hole for tax dollars. The United States spends more on its military than the next ten countries combined. While a strong defense is crucial, the sheer scale of spending raises questions about efficiency and necessity.

Overpriced contracts, failed weapons systems, and unaccounted-for funds are just a few examples of how defense spending can spiral out of control. It's like writing a blank check and hoping it's spent wisely, but often finding out it's been squandered.

Take the F-35 fighter jet program, for example. It's been plagued by cost overruns, delays, and technical issues, yet the spending continues. It's like buying a luxury car that constantly breaks down, but you keep paying for upgrades instead of cutting your losses. Defense spending is often justified as essential for national security, but the lack of oversight and accountability means billions of dollars can disappear without a trace.

Chapter 51: Subsidies for the Wealthy: Corporate Welfare Queens

Let's revisit subsidies for the wealthy – the corporate welfare queens. We've already touched on this in Part IV, but it's worth reiterating how these subsidies distort the market and benefit the rich at the expense of the average taxpayer.

While subsidies are supposed to promote economic growth, they often end up as handouts to already profitable corporations. It's like giving a billionaire a bonus check while the rest of us struggle to make ends meet. These subsidies create an uneven playing field, where small businesses can't compete with giants receiving government handouts. It's a system rigged to favor the wealthy, leaving the rest of us to pick up the slack.

Chapter 52: The Role of Lobbyists: Legislation for the Highest Bidder

Now, let's discuss the role of lobbyists – legislation for the highest bidder. Lobbyists are paid to influence lawmakers on behalf of special interest groups. And while lobbying is a legitimate part of the political process, it often skews legislation in favor of those with the deepest pockets.

From tax breaks for specific industries to loopholes for the wealthy, lobbyists ensure that the tax code is written with their clients in mind. It's like having a rulebook where the richest players get to make the rules. This creates a system where the needs of ordinary citizens are often overshadowed by the interests of the powerful.

Consider the fossil fuel industry. Despite the growing urgency to address climate change, fossil fuel companies spend millions on lobbying to maintain their tax breaks and subsidies. It's like paying someone to keep the status quo while the world burns. The influence of lobbyists ensures that tax legislation often serves the interests of the wealthy and powerful, leaving the rest of us to wonder if our voices will ever be heard.

Chapter 53: Political Contributions and Tax Breaks: The Vicious Cycle

Ladies and gentlemen, let's talk about political contributions and tax breaks – the vicious cycle. Political contributions buy influence, and that influence often results in tax breaks for the contributors. It's a pay-to-play system that undermines democracy and fairness.

Corporations and wealthy individuals donate large sums to political campaigns, and in return, they receive favorable tax treatment. It's like a revolving door where money and power circulate, leaving the rest of us outside looking in. This cycle perpetuates inequality and ensures that the tax code remains skewed in favor of the rich.

It's not just about buying influence; it's about shaping policy to benefit the donors. Tax breaks for industries like pharmaceuticals, oil, and tech are often the result of intense lobbying and political contributions. It's like having a VIP pass to the policymaking process, while the average citizen is stuck in the cheap seats.

Chapter 54: The Cost of Tax Enforcement: IRS Overreach

Finally, let's discuss the cost of tax enforcement – IRS overreach. The IRS is tasked with collecting taxes and ensuring compliance, but their methods can sometimes feel heavy-handed and invasive.

From aggressive audits to harsh penalties, the IRS's tactics can leave taxpayers feeling like they're under siege. It's like having a watchdog that occasionally bites the hand that feeds it. While tax enforcement is necessary, there's a fine line between ensuring compliance and overstepping boundaries.

For example, small businesses and self-employed individuals often bear the brunt of IRS scrutiny. It's easier for the IRS to target smaller entities than to take on multinational corporations with armies of lawyers. It's like going after the low-hanging fruit while the big players get away with tax avoidance. This approach can create a climate of fear and resentment, where honest taxpayers feel like they're being unfairly targeted.

In conclusion, folks, government and legislative influence play a significant role in shaping our tax system. From wasteful spending to the power of lobbyists, these factors ensure that the system remains skewed in favor of the wealthy and powerful. By understanding these dynamics, we can start to demand a fairer, more transparent system. So here's to uncovering the truth – may we one day see a tax system that works for everyone.

Part VII: Inequality and Social Impact

Chapter 55: Fueling Income Inequality: The Unfair Tax Burden

Ladies and gentlemen, let's start with a heavy hitter – fueling income inequality through the unfair tax burden. Our tax system is supposed to be progressive, meaning those who earn more should pay more. But in practice, it often ends up widening the gap between the rich and the poor.

Take the capital gains tax rate, for instance. Wealthy individuals who make their money through investments often pay a lower tax rate than those earning a regular salary. It's like playing a game where the rules are different depending on how much money you have. The rich get richer, and the rest of us are left to fight for the scraps.

And let's not forget about payroll taxes. These taxes are capped at a certain income level, meaning high earners stop paying them after reaching a threshold. Meanwhile, low- and middle-income workers pay a higher percentage of their income in payroll taxes. It's like a regressive tax disguised as a flat rate, disproportionately affecting those who can least afford it.

Chapter 56: Social Programs: Mismanagement of Your Contributions

Now, let's discuss social programs and the mismanagement of your contributions. We pay taxes with the expectation that the government will use them to fund essential services like education, healthcare, and social security. But all too often, these programs are plagued by inefficiency and waste.

Take the Supplemental Nutrition Assistance Program (SNAP), for example. While it's a lifeline for many, instances of fraud and mismanagement can undermine its effectiveness. It's like giving your money to a charity, only to find out a significant portion is being squandered. These inefficiencies mean less help for those who need it most and more taxpayer dollars down the drain.

And let's not forget about public infrastructure projects that go over budget and behind schedule. We expect our contributions to be used wisely, but too often, they're not. It's like paying for a five-star meal and getting a microwaved TV dinner instead.

Chapter 57: Tax Reform Scams: Empty Promises and Real Costs

Ladies and gentlemen, let's talk about tax reform scams – empty promises and real costs. Politicians love to talk about tax reform, promising to simplify the system and lower taxes for everyone. But in reality, many of these reforms end up benefiting the wealthy and powerful, leaving the rest of us to foot the bill.

Take the Tax Cuts and Jobs Act of 2017. It promised to boost the economy and put more money in the pockets of ordinary Americans. But in reality, the biggest beneficiaries were corporations and the wealthy. It's like being promised a feast and getting crumbs instead.

These so-called reforms often come with hidden costs, like increased deficits and cuts to essential services. It's a classic bait-and-switch, where the initial benefits are overshadowed by long-term consequences. We're left wondering if tax reform will ever truly serve the interests of the many instead of the few.

Chapter 58: The Social Security Trust Fund Myth: Ponzi Scheme or Not?

Now, let's revisit the Social Security Trust Fund – Ponzi scheme or not? We're told that our Social Security contributions are being saved in a trust fund for our retirement. But the reality is much murkier.

The money we pay into Social Security is used to pay current retirees, with any surplus being borrowed by the federal government to cover other expenses. It's a pay-as-you-go system, and as the population ages, the strain on this system becomes more and more apparent.

There's a real fear that Social Security won't be able to meet its obligations in the future, leaving younger generations wondering if they'll ever see a return on their contributions. It's like putting your money into a retirement plan, only to find out it's being spent faster than it's being saved. The trust fund might not be the Ponzi scheme some claim it to be, but it certainly has its challenges and vulnerabilities.

Chapter 59: The Flat Tax Fallacy: Simple Yet Deceptive

Ladies and gentlemen, let's talk about the flat tax fallacy – simple yet deceptive. The idea of a flat tax, where everyone pays the same percentage of their income, sounds appealing. It's straightforward, easy to understand, and seems fair on the surface. But dig a little deeper, and you'll find it's not as equitable as it appears.

A flat tax disproportionately benefits high-income earners, who would see their tax rates decrease, while low- and middle-income earners might end up paying more. It's like having everyone run the same race, but starting the wealthy at the halfway mark.

Moreover, a flat tax can lead to significant revenue shortfalls, forcing cuts to essential public services. It's like fixing a leaky roof by tearing down the house. Simplicity comes at a high cost, and it's usually the most vulnerable who pay the price.

Chapter 60: Whistleblowers' Plight: The Risk of Exposing Tax Fraud

Finally, let's discuss whistleblowers' plight – the risk of exposing tax fraud. Whistleblowers play a crucial role in uncovering tax evasion and fraud, but they often face significant personal and professional risks.

Exposing tax fraud can lead to retaliation, job loss, and legal battles. It's like being a canary in a coal mine, warning others of danger while risking your own well-being. Whistleblowers provide a vital public service, yet they often lack adequate protection and support.

And while there are laws designed to protect whistleblowers, enforcement is inconsistent, and the process can be lengthy and stressful. It's a system that relies on brave individuals to stand up against powerful interests, but it doesn't always have their back.

In conclusion, folks, the tax system is fraught with inequality and social impact issues that perpetuate disparities and hinder fairness. By understanding these challenges, we can start to demand a fairer, more transparent system. So here's to uncovering the truth – may we one day see a tax system that works for everyone.

Part VIII: Economic Sectors and Taxation

Chapter 61: Small Business Taxation: Stifling Growth and Innovation

Ladies and gentlemen, let's dive into the world of small business taxation – where dreams of entrepreneurship meet the harsh reality of the taxman. Small businesses are often hailed as the backbone of the economy, yet they face a tax burden that can stifle growth and innovation.

Unlike large corporations with armies of accountants, small businesses often struggle to navigate the complex tax code. It's like trying to play a game where the rules keep changing, and you don't have the playbook. The costs of compliance, from bookkeeping to filing taxes, can be overwhelming for small business owners, diverting time and resources away from innovation and growth.

Moreover, tax credits and deductions often favor larger companies. Small businesses are left scrambling to find the same advantages. It's like running a marathon with weights on your feet while your competitors are cruising on bikes. The result? Many small businesses either stay small or fold under the pressure, limiting their potential to contribute to the economy.

Chapter 62: Freelancers and the Gig Economy: Navigating the Tax Minefield

Now, let's talk about freelancers and the gig economy – the new frontier of work, but also a tax minefield. Freelancers, contractors, and gig workers enjoy the freedom and flexibility of their work, but they face unique tax challenges that can be daunting.

Unlike traditional employees, freelancers don't have taxes withheld from their paychecks. This means they need to make estimated tax payments throughout the year, a task that can be confusing and stressful. It's like navigating a maze with no map, hoping you're on the right path but never quite sure.

Freelancers also miss out on employer-provided benefits like health insurance and retirement contributions, making it even harder to save and plan for the future. The tax code doesn't make it any easier, with complex rules about deductible expenses, self-employment taxes, and business deductions. It's a system that feels like it's designed to trip you up at every turn.

Chapter 63: Consumer Debt: Taxation's Role in the Vicious Cycle

Ladies and gentlemen, let's discuss consumer debt – a vicious cycle exacerbated by taxation. High levels of consumer debt, from credit cards to student loans, are a reality for many Americans. And the tax system often makes it harder to break free from this cycle.

Interest on most consumer debt is not tax-deductible, meaning that while mortgage interest can provide a tax break, credit card interest and personal loans do not. This places a heavier burden on those struggling to manage their debts. It's like trying to climb out of a hole while someone keeps shoveling dirt back in.

Moreover, the tax system can penalize those who take early withdrawals from retirement accounts to pay off debt, imposing hefty penalties and taxes. It's a lose-lose situation where the efforts to become financially stable are met with more financial penalties. The result is a cycle of debt that's hard to escape, perpetuated by a tax system that doesn't provide relief where it's most needed.

Chapter 64: The Underground Economy: Ignored and Untaxed Wealth

Now, let's talk about the underground economy – ignored and untaxed wealth. The underground economy includes all the economic activities that go unreported and untaxed, from off-the-books labor to illegal activities. It's a shadow economy that operates outside the reach of the IRS.

While some people participate in the underground economy to avoid taxes, others do so because they have no choice. Undocumented workers, for example, often work in cash-based jobs that don't report income. This means billions of dollars in potential tax revenue are lost each year. It's like a hidden treasure that the taxman can't find.

The impact is significant. The loss of tax revenue means higher taxes for those who do comply, as well as underfunded public services. It's an unfair system where those playing by the rules are left to cover the shortfall created by those who don't. Addressing the underground economy is crucial for creating a fairer tax system, but it requires balancing enforcement with support for those forced into the shadows.

Chapter 65: Digital Economy Challenges: The Next Tax Frontier

Ladies and gentlemen, let's discuss the digital economy – the next tax frontier. As the digital economy grows, with e-commerce, remote work, and digital services, it presents new challenges for taxation. Traditional tax systems struggle to keep up with the rapidly changing digital landscape.

Companies like Amazon, Google, and Facebook operate globally, making it difficult for any single country to tax them effectively. These digital giants often shift profits to low-tax jurisdictions, avoiding higher taxes in the countries where they operate. It's like playing a game of whack-a-mole, where the profits keep disappearing just as you're about to catch them.

Consumers also face tax challenges in the digital economy. Sales tax on online purchases varies widely, creating confusion and compliance issues. As more services move online, from streaming to remote work, figuring out how to tax these transactions fairly and effectively becomes increasingly complex.

Chapter 66: Cryptocurrency Confusion: Taxing the Digital Revolution

Now, let's talk about cryptocurrency – the Wild West of the financial world, and a new challenge for taxation. Cryptocurrencies like Bitcoin and Ethereum operate outside traditional financial systems, creating confusion for both taxpayers and the IRS.

The IRS treats cryptocurrencies as property, meaning that each transaction is a taxable event. This makes using crypto for everyday purchases a nightmare of record-keeping. Imagine having to track and report the gains or losses for every cup of coffee you buy with Bitcoin. It's like trying to keep track of every breath you take.

Moreover, the anonymity and decentralization of cryptocurrencies make enforcement difficult. While the IRS has taken steps to crack down on unreported crypto income, it's still a cat-and-mouse game with savvy users finding ways to stay ahead. The digital revolution in finance is here, but the tax system is struggling to catch up.

Chapter 67: Consumption Tax Proposals: Shifting the Burden

Ladies and gentlemen, let's discuss consumption tax proposals – shifting the burden of taxation. A consumption tax, such as a national sales tax or value-added tax (VAT), taxes spending rather than income. Proponents argue that it's simpler and encourages saving and investment. But it's not without its controversies.

A consumption tax can be regressive, hitting lower-income individuals harder since they spend a larger portion of their income on necessities. It's like charging a toll on the only bridge in town – everyone has to cross it, but the poor feel the pinch more than the rich.

Moreover, implementing a national consumption tax could lead to significant price increases, affecting consumer behavior and potentially slowing economic growth. It's a balancing act between simplicity and fairness, and finding the right approach is a challenge.

Chapter 68: VAT vs. Sales Tax: Global Comparisons and Local Implications

Finally, let's talk about VAT vs. sales tax – global comparisons and local implications. Both VAT and sales tax are consumption taxes, but they operate differently. A VAT is collected at each stage of production and distribution, while a sales tax is collected only at the point of sale to the final consumer.

Many countries around the world use VAT, finding it to be a more efficient way to raise revenue. However, implementing VAT in the US would require a significant overhaul of the current tax system. It's like switching from driving on the right side of the road to the left – it's possible, but it's a massive adjustment.

Sales tax, on the other hand, is simpler but can be more prone to evasion and less stable as a revenue source. The choice between VAT and sales tax involves trade-offs between efficiency, simplicity, and fairness. It's a complex decision with far-reaching implications for both the economy and everyday consumers.

In conclusion, folks, the tax system's impact on different economic sectors reveals a web of challenges and inequalities. By understanding these issues, we can start to demand a fairer, more transparent system. So here's to uncovering the truth – may we one day see a tax system that works for everyone.

Part IX: Future and Emerging Tax Issues

Chapter 69: Digital Economy Challenges: The Next Tax Frontier

Ladies and gentlemen, let's start with the digital economy – the next tax frontier. As we increasingly move our lives online, the digital economy is booming, but our tax system is struggling to keep up. Companies like Amazon, Google, and Facebook operate on a global scale, making it difficult for any single country to tax them effectively.

These tech giants often shift profits to low-tax jurisdictions, avoiding higher taxes in the countries where they actually do business. It's like trying to nail jelly to a wall – just when you think you've got it, it slips away. This profit-shifting game leaves governments scrambling to reclaim lost revenue, often at the expense of smaller, less mobile businesses.

Consumers, too, face new challenges. The rise of e-commerce has complicated sales tax collection. Depending on where you live and where you buy from, the tax rules can be as clear as mud. It's a brave new world, and our tax policies need to adapt to ensure fairness and efficiency in this digital age.

Chapter 70: Cryptocurrency Confusion: Taxing the Digital Revolution

Now, let's talk about cryptocurrency – the Wild West of the financial world and a new challenge for taxation. Cryptocurrencies like Bitcoin and Ethereum operate outside traditional financial systems, creating confusion for both taxpayers and the IRS.

The IRS treats cryptocurrencies as property, meaning each transaction is a taxable event. Imagine having to track and report gains or losses every time you buy a cup of coffee with Bitcoin. It's like trying to keep track of every grain of sand at the beach.

Moreover, the anonymity and decentralization of cryptocurrencies make enforcement difficult. While the IRS is stepping up efforts to ensure compliance, it's still a game of cat and mouse. The digital revolution in finance is here, but the tax system is struggling to catch up, leaving both users and regulators in a state of flux.

Chapter 71: Consumption Tax Proposals: Shifting the Burden

Ladies and gentlemen, let's discuss consumption tax proposals – shifting the burden of taxation. A consumption tax, such as a national sales tax or value-added tax (VAT), taxes spending rather than income. Proponents argue that it's simpler and encourages saving and investment, but it's not without controversy.

A consumption tax can be regressive, hitting lower-income individuals harder since they spend a larger portion of their income on necessities. It's like charging a toll on the only bridge in town – everyone has to cross it, but the poor feel the pinch more than the rich.

Moreover, implementing a national consumption tax could lead to significant price increases, affecting consumer behavior and potentially slowing economic growth. It's a balancing act between simplicity and fairness, and finding the right approach is a challenge that requires careful consideration.

Chapter 72: VAT vs. Sales Tax: Global Comparisons and Local Implications

Let's talk about VAT vs. sales tax – global comparisons and local implications. Both VAT and sales tax are consumption taxes, but they operate differently. A VAT is collected at each stage of production and distribution, while a sales tax is collected only at the point of sale to the final consumer.

Many countries around the world use VAT, finding it to be a more efficient way to raise revenue. However, implementing VAT in the US would require a significant overhaul of the current tax system. It's like switching from driving on the right side of the road to the left – it's possible, but it's a massive adjustment.

Sales tax, on the other hand, is simpler but can be more prone to evasion and less stable as a revenue source. The choice between VAT and sales tax involves trade-offs between efficiency, simplicity, and fairness. It's a complex decision with far-reaching implications for both the economy and everyday consumers.

Chapter 73: Tax Evasion vs. Tax Avoidance: The Legal Grey Areas

Ladies and gentlemen, let's dive into tax evasion vs. tax avoidance – the legal grey areas. Tax evasion is illegal, involving deliberate actions to misrepresent income or hide money. Tax avoidance, on the other hand, involves using legal means to minimize tax liability, often exploiting loopholes in the tax code.

While tax evasion is clearly wrong and punishable by law, tax avoidance occupies a murkier space. Corporations and wealthy individuals often employ armies of accountants and lawyers to navigate the tax code, finding ways to reduce their tax bills. It's like playing a game of chess where only some players know all the rules.

This distinction can create a sense of injustice, as ordinary taxpayers feel the weight of their tax obligations while the rich and powerful seemingly play by a different set of rules. Addressing this issue requires closing loopholes and ensuring that the tax code is fair and transparent, leveling the playing field for everyone.

Chapter 74: Whistleblowers and the Fight Against Tax Fraud

Now, let's discuss whistleblowers and the fight against tax fraud. Whistleblowers play a crucial role in exposing tax evasion and fraud, often at great personal risk. They are the unsung heroes who help ensure that everyone pays their fair share.

Exposing tax fraud can lead to retaliation, job loss, and lengthy legal battles. It's like being a canary in a coal mine, warning others of danger while risking your own safety. While there are laws designed to protect whistleblowers, enforcement is inconsistent, and the process can be daunting.

Whistleblowers need robust protections and support to continue their vital work. Recognizing their contributions and ensuring they are not penalized for their bravery is essential in the fight against tax fraud. They help shine a light on the dark corners of the tax system, making it fairer for everyone.

Chapter 75: Global Tax Coordination: Tackling International Tax Challenges

Ladies and gentlemen, let's talk about global tax coordination – tackling international tax challenges. In an increasingly interconnected world, tax issues don't stop at national borders. Multinational corporations and digital businesses operate globally, creating challenges for individual countries trying to tax them fairly.

International tax coordination involves efforts to harmonize tax rules and combat tax avoidance and evasion on a global scale. Initiatives like the OECD's Base Erosion and Profit

Shifting (BEPS) project aim to address these issues, but achieving consensus among nations is no small feat. It's like trying to get a room full of cats to agree on one bowl of food.

Global tax coordination is essential to prevent a race to the bottom, where countries compete to offer the lowest tax rates to attract business, undermining their own revenue bases. It's a complex dance that requires cooperation and compromise to ensure a fair and effective tax system worldwide.

Chapter 76: The Future of Work: Taxing Remote and Gig Workers

Now, let's discuss the future of work – taxing remote and gig workers. The rise of remote work and the gig economy has transformed how we work, but the tax system is still playing catch-up. Traditional tax rules don't always fit the new realities of a digital and flexible workforce.

Remote workers may face tax issues related to working across state or even international borders. Determining where income is earned and where taxes should be paid can be complicated. It's like trying to solve a puzzle with pieces from different boxes.

Gig workers, on the other hand, often don't have taxes withheld from their earnings, leading to challenges in estimating and paying taxes. The lack of employer-provided benefits also means additional financial responsibilities. Adapting the tax system to these new work arrangements is crucial for ensuring fairness and compliance.

Chapter 77: Environmental Taxes: Incentivizing Green Practices

Ladies and gentlemen, let's talk about environmental taxes – incentivizing green practices. Environmental taxes aim to reduce pollution and promote sustainable behavior by taxing activities that harm the environment. It's a way to use the tax system to drive positive change.

Taxes on carbon emissions, plastic bags, and other pollutants can encourage businesses and individuals to adopt greener practices. It's like using a carrot and stick approach to nudge us towards a more sustainable future. However, the design of these taxes is crucial to their success. They need to be set at a level that truly incentivizes change without placing an undue burden on low-income households.

Revenue from environmental taxes can be used to fund renewable energy projects, conservation efforts, and other green initiatives, creating a virtuous cycle. It's about aligning economic incentives with environmental goals to build a better future for all.

Chapter 78: The Aging Population: Tax Implications of Demographic Shifts

Finally, let's discuss the aging population – the tax implications of demographic shifts. As the population ages, the tax system faces new challenges in funding retirement and healthcare benefits for a growing number of elderly citizens.

An aging population means a smaller workforce supporting a larger retired population. This demographic shift can strain social security systems and increase healthcare costs, requiring adjustments to tax policies to ensure sustainability. It's like trying to balance a seesaw with a shifting weight distribution.

Policymakers need to consider how to adapt the tax system to address these challenges, whether through adjustments to payroll taxes, retirement benefits, or other measures. Ensuring that the tax system remains fair and capable of supporting an aging population is essential for long-term economic stability.

In conclusion, folks, the future and emerging tax issues reveal a landscape full of challenges and opportunities. By understanding these issues, we can start to demand a fairer, more transparent system that adapts to our changing world. So here's to uncovering the truth – may we one day see a tax system that works for everyone.

Part X: Why You Shouldn't Pay Taxes

Chapter 79: The Moral Argument: Taxation as Theft

Ladies and gentlemen, let's dive into a contentious topic – the moral argument against paying taxes. Some people view taxation as a form of theft, arguing that it's morally wrong for the government to take a portion of their hard-earned money without explicit consent.

Imagine working tirelessly all year, only to have a chunk of your paycheck taken away. It's like having a pickpocket who doesn't even bother to hide. The moral argument hinges on the belief that individuals have a right to the fruits of their labor and that any coercive taking of that property is inherently unjust. While this perspective is contentious and certainly not universally accepted, it raises important questions about consent and the legitimacy of government authority.

Chapter 80: Historical Precedents for Tax Resistance

Now, let's discuss historical precedents for tax resistance. Throughout history, people have resisted taxes they deemed unfair or oppressive. From the Boston Tea Party to modern tax protests, tax resistance has played a crucial role in shaping political and economic systems.

The Boston Tea Party of 1773 is a classic example. Colonists protested the British government's tax on tea, leading to the American Revolution. It's like saying, "No taxation without representation!" and backing it up with action. Fast forward to modern times, and we see movements like the Tea Party in the United States, which emerged in response to perceived excessive taxation and government spending.

These historical examples demonstrate that tax resistance isn't just about avoiding payments – it's often about challenging broader issues of governance, representation, and fairness. They remind us that questioning and challenging the tax system has been a part of democratic evolution.

Chapter 81: Inefficiency and Waste: Where Your Money Really Goes

Ladies and gentlemen, let's talk about inefficiency and waste – where your tax money really goes. One of the most compelling arguments against paying taxes is the inefficiency and waste within government spending.

Imagine giving your money to a friend who promises to use it wisely but instead spends it on unnecessary gadgets and overpriced meals. That's how many people feel about the government. From billion-dollar defense contracts for equipment that never gets used to costly public projects that go over budget and behind schedule, wasteful spending is a significant concern.

When taxpayers see their money being squandered on inefficiencies and mismanagement, it fuels frustration and skepticism about the value of their contributions. It's like filling up a leaky bucket – no matter how much you pour in, it never seems to fill up.

Chapter 82: Alternative Funding Models: Voluntary Contributions

Now, let's explore alternative funding models – voluntary contributions. What if instead of mandatory taxes, we funded government services through voluntary contributions? It sounds radical, but some argue that it could lead to more efficient and accountable government spending.

Imagine a system where you choose where your money goes, like crowdfunding your favorite government projects. It's like donating to a charity – you support causes you believe in and see the direct impact of your contributions. This model relies on the belief that people will willingly fund essential services if they see the value and effectiveness of those services.

While voluntary contributions face significant challenges, such as ensuring adequate funding for less popular but essential services, the idea highlights the potential for increased transparency and accountability in government spending.

Chapter 83: The Right to Protest: Civil Disobedience and Taxes

Ladies and gentlemen, let's discuss the right to protest – civil disobedience and taxes. Tax resistance can be seen as a form of civil disobedience, where individuals refuse to pay taxes to protest government policies or actions they consider unjust.

Think of it as a peaceful way to say, "I'm mad as hell, and I'm not going to take it anymore!" Civil disobedience has a long history, from Henry David Thoreau's refusal to pay taxes in protest of slavery and the Mexican-American War to modern-day movements against military spending or climate inaction.

By refusing to pay taxes, individuals can draw attention to issues and spark public debate. While this form of protest carries legal risks, it underscores the power of individuals to challenge and seek change within their governments. It's a reminder that sometimes, standing up for what you believe in requires bold and courageous actions.

Chapter 84: The Case for Tax-Free Zones: Economic and Social Benefits

Now, let's explore the case for tax-free zones – areas where taxes are minimized or eliminated to stimulate economic growth and social benefits. Tax-free zones, also known as economic free zones, aim to attract businesses and investors by offering favorable tax conditions.

Imagine a city where businesses thrive, jobs are plentiful, and innovation flourishes because taxes are low or nonexistent. It's like creating a fertile ground where the seeds of economic prosperity can grow without the weeds of heavy taxation. These zones can lead to job creation, increased investment, and economic revitalization of regions that might otherwise struggle.

While tax-free zones can drive economic growth, they also raise questions about fairness and equity. The benefits often need to be weighed against potential downsides, such as reduced government revenue and the impact on surrounding areas. However, they present an intriguing model for stimulating economic activity.

Chapter 85: Tax Revolts: Historical and Modern Examples

Ladies and gentlemen, let's talk about tax revolts – historical and modern examples of people pushing back against taxation. From the Whiskey Rebellion in the 1790s to the modern anti-tax movements, tax revolts have been a powerful force for change.

The Whiskey Rebellion saw farmers in western Pennsylvania protest an excise tax on whiskey. It was like a spirited response to what they saw as an unjust burden, and it tested the young American government's ability to enforce tax laws. In more recent times, movements like the Tea Party have mobilized people against what they view as excessive taxation and government overreach.

These revolts and movements highlight the tensions that can arise when people feel overburdened by taxes. They also demonstrate the potential for collective action to influence tax policy and governance.

Chapter 86: The Psychological Impact: Stress and Financial Strain

Now, let's discuss the psychological impact of taxes – stress and financial strain. The tax system isn't just a financial burden; it can also take a significant toll on mental health.

Imagine the anxiety of facing a complex tax return, worrying about audits, and feeling the strain of making ends meet while paying a substantial portion of your income in taxes. It's like carrying an invisible weight that affects your well-being. The stress of tax season, coupled with the fear of penalties and audits, can lead to significant anxiety and financial strain.

For many people, the tax burden contributes to a cycle of stress and financial insecurity. Addressing these psychological impacts is crucial for creating a tax system that is not only fair but also supportive of mental health and well-being.

Chapter 87: The Hidden Costs: Compliance and Preparation

Ladies and gentlemen, let's talk about the hidden costs of taxes – compliance and preparation. Filing taxes isn't just about paying your dues; it also involves significant time, effort, and often money to ensure compliance.

Think about the hours spent gathering receipts, filling out forms, and possibly hiring professionals to help navigate the complexities of the tax code. It's like having a second job that you didn't apply for but can't quit. The costs of tax preparation services, software, and even the time spent can add up, creating a substantial hidden tax burden.

Simplifying the tax code and reducing these compliance costs could make the tax system more efficient and less stressful for everyone. It's about finding ways to streamline the process and reduce the hidden costs that weigh on taxpayers.

Chapter 88: The Wealth Inequality Argument: Taxes Perpetuating Disparities

Now, let's discuss the wealth inequality argument – how taxes can perpetuate disparities. While taxes are often seen as a way to redistribute wealth, the current system can sometimes reinforce inequality rather than alleviate it.

Wealthy individuals and corporations have the resources to exploit loopholes and reduce their tax burden, while lower-income individuals often bear a higher relative burden. It's like a game where the rich get to play by different rules. This disparity can lead to a concentration of wealth and power, exacerbating social and economic inequalities.

Addressing these disparities requires closing loopholes, ensuring progressive taxation, and implementing policies that promote economic mobility and fairness. It's about creating a tax system that truly levels the playing field.

Chapter 89: Sovereign Citizen Movement: A Radical Approach

Ladies and gentlemen, let's talk about the sovereign citizen movement – a radical approach to tax resistance. Sovereign citizens believe that they are not subject to government authority, including tax laws. It's a controversial and extreme stance, but one that has garnered attention and followers.

Imagine declaring yourself free from all government rules and regulations, including taxes. It's like stepping into a parallel universe where the rules don't apply. While the movement is often associated with legal battles and confrontations with authorities, it highlights deep-seated frustrations with government and taxation.

The sovereign citizen movement raises important questions about governance, authority, and the legitimacy of tax systems. While their methods are extreme, the underlying concerns about government overreach and taxation are shared by many.

Chapter 90: The Path to Fair Taxation: Solutions and Reforms

Finally, let's discuss the path to fair taxation – solutions and reforms. Addressing the issues and arguments against paying taxes requires comprehensive reforms that create a fairer, more transparent, and efficient tax system.

Potential solutions include simplifying the tax code, closing loopholes, ensuring progressive taxation, and improving transparency and accountability in government spending. It's like building a new house on a solid foundation, ensuring stability and fairness for all.

Reforming the tax system is no small task, but it's essential for addressing the frustrations and challenges faced by taxpayers. By creating a system that is fair, transparent, and efficient, we can restore trust and ensure that everyone pays their fair share.

In conclusion, folks, the arguments against paying taxes reveal deep-seated frustrations and challenges within our current system. By understanding these issues and exploring potential solutions, we can work towards a fairer, more equitable tax system. So here's to uncovering the truth – may we one day see a tax system that works for everyone.

Part XI: Conclusion and Solutions

Chapter 91: Inflation and Taxes: Eroding Your Purchasing Power

Ladies and gentlemen, let's dive into the first topic of our conclusion – inflation and taxes. Inflation is the silent thief that erodes your purchasing power over time, and when combined with taxes, it can feel like a double whammy.

Imagine working hard and saving diligently, only to find that your money buys less and less each year. It's like running on a treadmill that keeps speeding up while you're trying to keep pace. Inflation reduces the real value of your income and savings, while taxes take a chunk of what's left. The impact is particularly harsh on those with fixed incomes, such as retirees who see their purchasing power decline while their tax burdens remain unchanged or even increase.

To address this, it's crucial to adjust tax brackets for inflation regularly, ensuring that taxpayers don't end up paying more simply because of rising prices. Additionally, protecting savings and investments from inflationary erosion through tax-advantaged accounts can help individuals preserve their wealth.

Chapter 92: Municipal Taxes: The Local Double Dip

Next, let's discuss municipal taxes – the local double dip. Municipal taxes, such as property taxes, sales taxes, and local income taxes, are additional layers on top of state and federal taxes. It's like ordering a hamburger and getting charged extra for every topping, whether you wanted them or not.

Municipal taxes fund essential local services like schools, police, and infrastructure, but they can also create significant financial burdens for residents. High property taxes, for instance, can make homeownership unaffordable for many. It's like owning a home but renting it from the government, with the rent increasing every year.

Reforming municipal tax systems to ensure they are fair, transparent, and proportional to the ability to pay can help alleviate these burdens. Encouraging efficiency and accountability in local government spending can also ensure that tax dollars are used wisely.

Chapter 93: State vs. Federal Taxes: Redundant and Burdensome

Now, let's talk about the interplay between state and federal taxes – redundant and burdensome. Taxpayers often face a confusing array of state and federal taxes, each with its own rules, rates, and filing requirements. It's like playing a game with two sets of rules that don't always align.

This complexity creates administrative burdens and increases the risk of errors and penalties. For businesses operating in multiple states, it's even more complicated, requiring extensive resources to ensure compliance with varying state tax laws. It's like trying to navigate a maze with a different map for each section.

Simplifying and harmonizing state and federal tax codes could reduce these burdens and make compliance easier. Streamlining the tax system would save time and money for taxpayers and the government alike, making the system more efficient and user-friendly.

Chapter 94: Tax Evasion vs. Tax Avoidance: The Legal Grey Areas

Ladies and gentlemen, let's delve into tax evasion vs. tax avoidance – the legal grey areas. Tax evasion is illegal and involves deliberately misrepresenting income or hiding money to avoid taxes. Tax avoidance, on the other hand, involves using legal means to minimize tax liability, often by exploiting loopholes.

While tax evasion is clearly wrong and punishable by law, tax avoidance occupies a murkier space. Wealthy individuals and corporations often employ sophisticated strategies to reduce their tax bills, taking advantage of complex and sometimes obscure provisions in the tax code. It's like playing a game of chess where only some players know all the rules.

Addressing this issue requires closing loopholes and ensuring that the tax code is clear and fair. It's about creating a system where everyone pays their fair share, and there are no hidden tricks to exploit.

Chapter 95: Conclusion: Finding a Path to Fair Taxation

Ladies and gentlemen, we've reached the grand finale – finding a path to fair taxation. The journey through our tax system has highlighted numerous issues and challenges, but it has also provided insights into potential solutions.

Creating a fair tax system involves simplifying the tax code, closing loopholes, ensuring progressive taxation, and improving transparency and accountability in government spending. It's about building a system that is fair, efficient, and capable of adapting to our changing world.

We need to address the root causes of inequality and ensure that everyone pays their fair share. By focusing on fairness, transparency, and efficiency, we can create a tax system that works for everyone, not just the wealthy and powerful. It's about restoring trust and ensuring that the system is designed to serve the needs of all citizens.

Chapter 96: Appendix: Resources and References

Finally, let's talk about the appendix – resources and references. In this section, you'll find a wealth of information to help you navigate the complex world of taxation. From government publications to expert analyses, these resources provide valuable insights and guidance.

The appendix includes links to key government agencies, tax preparation tools, and organizations advocating for tax reform. It's like having a toolkit to help you understand and manage your tax obligations. Whether you're a seasoned taxpayer or just starting out, these resources can provide the support you need to make informed decisions.

In conclusion, folks, the path to a fairer tax system is challenging but essential. By understanding the issues and exploring potential solutions, we can work towards a system that is fair, transparent, and efficient. So here's to uncovering the truth – may we one day see a tax system that works for everyone. Thank you for joining me on this journey, and let's continue to strive for a better future.

BONUS CHAPTER

Part XII: Strategies for Minimizing Tax Burden

Chapter 81: Business Ownership: Maximizing Deductions and Tax Benefits

Owning a business provides numerous opportunities to reduce your tax liability. Here's how you can leverage business ownership for tax benefits:

Example: Deducting Business Expenses

- **Office Supplies:** Keep receipts for all office supplies purchased, as these are fully deductible.
- **Travel Expenses:** Deduct the cost of business-related travel, including airfare, lodging, and meals.
- **Home Office Deduction:** If you use a part of your home exclusively for business, you can deduct a portion of your home expenses, like rent or mortgage interest and utilities.

By keeping detailed records and understanding what qualifies as a deductible expense, you can significantly reduce your taxable income.

Chapter 82: Roth IRA: Tax-Free Growth and Withdrawals

A Roth IRA offers tax-free growth and withdrawals, making it a powerful tool for tax planning.

Example:

- **Tax-Free Growth:** Contributions to a Roth IRA are made with after-tax dollars, but the investments grow tax-free. If you invest $5,000 annually and it grows to $100,000, you won't owe taxes on the gains.
- **Tax-Free Withdrawals:** Withdrawals in retirement are tax-free, providing tax-free income when you might be in a higher tax bracket.

By contributing to a Roth IRA, you can build a tax-free retirement nest egg.

Chapter 83: Municipal Bonds: Tax-Free Interest Income

Investing in municipal bonds can provide tax-free interest income.

Example:

- **Tax-Free Interest:** Interest earned from municipal bonds is typically exempt from federal income tax and, in some cases, state and local taxes. If you invest $10,000 in municipal bonds with a 3% interest rate, you'll earn $300 tax-free annually.

Municipal bonds are a great way to earn tax-free income, particularly for those in higher tax brackets.

Chapter 84: Capital Gains Taxes: Timing and Holding Periods

Managing capital gains taxes involves strategic planning of when to sell investments.

Example:

- **Long-Term vs. Short-Term Gains:** Holding an asset for more than a year qualifies for lower long-term capital gains tax rates. If you buy stock for $1,000 and sell it for $1,500 after a year, you'll pay a lower rate on the $500 gain compared to selling it within a year.

By timing your sales to benefit from lower long-term capital gains rates, you can reduce your tax liability.

Chapter 85: Tax Loss Harvesting: Turning Losses into Gains

Tax loss harvesting involves selling losing investments to offset gains.

Example:

- **Offset Gains:** If you have a $1,000 gain on one stock and a $1,000 loss on another, selling the losing stock can offset the gain, resulting in no taxable capital gain.
- **Carry Forward Losses:** If your losses exceed gains, you can carry forward the losses to future years to offset future gains.

This strategy can help you manage and reduce your overall tax liability on investments.

Chapter 86: Buying a Home Using OPM (Other People's Money)

Buying a home with minimal personal investment can offer tax benefits.

Example:

- **Mortgage Interest Deduction:** If you buy a home using a mortgage, you can deduct the interest paid on the loan. For a $300,000 mortgage at 4% interest, the interest deduction in the first year could be around $12,000.
- **Property Tax Deduction:** Property taxes are also deductible, adding to the tax benefits of homeownership.

Using OPM to buy a home allows you to leverage deductions while building equity.

Chapter 87: Home Sale Exemptions for Different Price Ranges

When you sell your home, you may qualify for tax exemptions on the gain.

Example:

- **Primary Residence Exclusion:** Single filers can exclude up to $250,000, and married couples up to $500,000, of the gain from the sale of a primary residence. If you bought a home for $200,000 and sold it for $450,000, the $250,000 gain would be tax-free for single filers.

This exemption helps homeowners avoid paying taxes on the appreciation of their primary residence.

Chapter 88: Depreciation: Cars, Homes, and Rental Property

Depreciation allows you to deduct the cost of an asset over its useful life.

Example:

- **Cars:** Business owners can depreciate vehicles used for business purposes. If you buy a car for $30,000, you can deduct a portion of the cost each year.
- **Homes:** While personal homes aren't depreciable, rental properties are. If you buy a rental property for $300,000, you can depreciate it over 27.5 years, resulting in an annual deduction of approximately $10,909.
- **Rental Property:** Depreciating rental properties can offset rental income, reducing your taxable income.

Depreciation helps manage and lower taxable income over time by spreading the cost of an asset.

Chapter 89: Tax Returns with Children: Credits and Deductions

Having children can provide significant tax benefits through credits and deductions.

Example:

- **Child Tax Credit:** This credit offers up to $2,000 per child under 17, directly reducing your tax bill.
- **Child and Dependent Care Credit:** If you pay for childcare, you can claim a credit for a portion of those expenses, up to $3,000 for one child or $6,000 for two or more children.
- **Education Credits:** The American Opportunity Credit offers up to $2,500 per student for higher education expenses.

These credits and deductions can significantly reduce your tax liability if you have children.

Chapter 90: Best States for Taxes: Maximizing State Tax Benefits

Choosing the right state to live in can offer substantial tax advantages.

Example:

- **No State Income Tax:** States like Florida, Texas, and Nevada do not impose state income tax, which can save you a significant amount of money.
- **Low Property Taxes:** States like Hawaii and Alabama have some of the lowest property taxes in the country.
- **Sales Tax:** States like Oregon and New Hampshire do not have a state sales tax.

By choosing a state with favorable tax policies, you can minimize your overall tax burden.

Chapter 91: State Tax Benefits: Taking Advantage of Each State

Understanding and utilizing state-specific tax benefits can further reduce your tax liability.

Example:

- **State-Specific Credits:** Some states offer unique tax credits, such as California's solar energy credit or New York's tuition credit.
- **Retirement Income Exemptions:** States like Pennsylvania and Mississippi do not tax retirement income, benefiting retirees.
- **Homestead Exemptions:** Many states offer property tax reductions for primary residences, known as homestead exemptions.

By researching and taking advantage of state-specific tax benefits, you can optimize your tax strategy and maximize savings.

In conclusion, folks, there are numerous strategies for minimizing your tax burden and keeping more of your hard-earned money. By understanding and utilizing these techniques, you can create a tax-efficient financial plan that supports your goals and ensures long-term success. So here's to smart tax planning – may we all find ways to maximize our wealth and minimize our taxes!

Index

A

- AMT (Alternative Minimum Tax): 20, 70
- Appendix: Resources and References: 91
- Audit Anxiety: Living Under IRS Threat: 22, 32

B

- Business Expenses: Optimizing Write-Offs: 76
- Business Ownership: Maximizing Deductions and Tax Benefits: 81
- Buying a Home Using OPM (Other People's Money): 86

C

- Capital Gains Strategies: Timing and Holding Periods: 72
- Capital Gains Taxes: Penalizing Your Investments: 7, 85
- Case for Tax-Free Zones: Economic and Social Benefits: 85
- Charitable Giving: Philanthropy with Benefits: 75
- Child and Dependent Care Credit: 89
- Child Tax Credit: 89
- Conclusion: Finding a Path to Fair Taxation: 95
- Consumer Debt: Taxation's Role in the Vicious Cycle: 40

- Corporate Tax Evasion: Multinational Manipulation: 17, 27

D

- Depreciation: Cars, Homes, and Rental Property: 88
- Depreciation: Cars: 88
- Depreciation: Rental Property: 88
- Defense Spending: Tax Dollars into a Black Hole: 27, 50
- Digital Economy Challenges: The Next Tax Frontier: 42, 69

E

- Educational Impact: Student Loan Tax Deduction Deceptions: 23, 33
- Estate Planning: Reducing Future Tax Burdens: 77
- Estate Taxes: Death's Financial Sting: 10
- Environmental Taxes: Greenwashing Your Wallet: 15
- Environmental Taxes: Incentivizing Green Practices: 77
- Executive Summary: 1

F

- Flat Tax Fallacy: Simple Yet Deceptive: 36
- Fueling Income Inequality: The Unfair Tax Burden: 32

G

- Gift Taxes: The Hidden Cost of Generosity: 11
- Global Tax Coordination: Tackling International Tax Challenges: 48
- Government Waste: Funding Inefficiency with Your Money: 26, 49

H

- Healthcare Taxes: The Hidden Costs of Illness: 24, 34
- Hidden and Indirect Taxes: 13
- Hidden Costs: Compliance and Preparation: 90
- Home Sale Exemptions for Different Price Ranges: 87

I

- Income Tax: Birth and Historical Scam: 2
- Inflation and Taxes: Eroding Your Purchasing Power: 91
- Inefficiency and Waste: Where Your Money Really Goes: 54

J

- Job-Related Deductions: 5

L

- Lobbyists: Role and Influence: 29, 52

- Loopholes for the Rich: The Legal Evaders: 16

M

- Marriage Penalty: Taxing Your Union: 21, 31
- Municipal Bonds: Tax-Free Interest Income: 83
- Municipal Taxes: The Local Double Dip: 65

N

- National Tax Coordination: 69

O

- Offshore Tax Haven Scandal: Hiding Wealth Overseas: 19
- OPM (Other People's Money): 86

P

- Payroll Taxes: Double Dipping into Your Earnings: 6
- Political Contributions and Tax Breaks: The Vicious Cycle: 30, 53
- Property Taxes: The Homeownership Trap: 9

R

- Retirement Accounts: Tax-Advantaged Savings: 82
- Roth IRA: Tax-Free Growth and Withdrawals: 82

S

- Sales Tax: The Sneaky Wallet Drainer: 8
- Small Business Taxation: Stifling Growth and Innovation: 38
- Social Programs: Mismanagement of Your Contributions: 33
- Social Security Trust Fund Myth: Ponzi Scheme or Not?: 35, 58
- Sovereign Citizen Movement: A Radical Approach: 89
- State Tax Benefits: Taking Advantage of Each State: 90
- State vs. Federal Taxes: Redundant and Burdensome: 66
- Student Loan Tax Deduction Deceptions: 23, 33
- Subsidies for the Wealthy: Corporate Welfare Queens: 18, 28, 51

T

- Tax Avoidance: Legal Grey Areas: 46, 67
- Tax Brackets: Punishing Your Success: 4
- Tax Credits: Leveraging Every Opportunity: 71
- Tax Deduction Deceptions: Educational Impact: 23, 33
- Tax Deductions: Maximizing Your Write-Offs: 81
- Tax Evasion: Legal Grey Areas: 46, 67
- Tax Loss Harvesting: Turning Losses into Gains: 73
- Tax Preparation Costs: Paying to Pay Taxes: 25, 90

- Tax Reform Scams: Empty Promises and Real Costs: 34
- Tax Returns: Benefits if You Have Children: 89
- Tax Returns: Benefits if Your Children Go to School or Daycare: 89
- Tax-Free Growth and Withdrawals: Roth IRA: 82
- Tax-Free Interest Income: Municipal Bonds: 83

U

- Underground Economy: Ignored and Untaxed Wealth: 41

V

- VAT vs. Sales Tax: Global Comparisons and Local Implications: 45, 70

W

- Wealth Inequality Argument: Taxes Perpetuating Disparities: 88
- Whistleblowers' Plight: Risk of Exposing Tax Fraud: 37
- Whistleblowers and Tax Fraud: 47

www.ingramcontent.com/pod-product-compliance
Lightning Source LLC
Chambersburg PA
CBHW072003210526
45479CB00003B/1044